Lara

On your 10th Birthday with ♡

from Mommy and Daddy

S0-BDL-617

On your 10th Birthday with ♡

from Mommy and Daddy

KAREN KAIN
LADY of DANCE

David Street

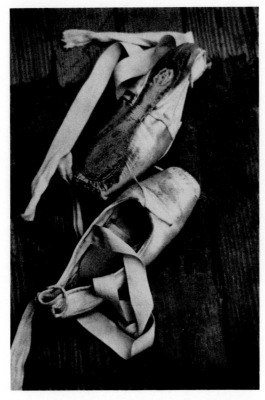

Text by David Mason

McGraw-Hill Ryerson Limited

Toronto   Montreal   New York   St. Louis   San Francisco   Auckland   Beirut   Bogotá
Düsseldorf   Johannesburg   Lisbon   London   Lucerne   Madrid   Mexico   New Delhi
Panama   Paris   San Juan   São Paulo   Singapore   Sydney   Tokyo

KAREN KAIN, LADY OF DANCE
Copyright © McGraw-Hill Ryerson Limited, 1978. All rights
reserved. No part of this publication may be reproduced, stored in a
retrieval system or transmitted in any form or by any means,
electronic, mechanical, photocopying, recording, or otherwise,
without the prior written permission of McGraw-Hill Ryerson Limited.

ISBN 0-07-082705-2

  2 3 4 5 6 7 8 9   **BP**   7 6 5 4 3 2 1 0 9 8

Printed and bound in Canada

Canadian Cataloguing in Publication Data

Street, David, date
  Karen Kain

ISBN 0-07-082705-2

1. Kain, Karen, 1951–   — Portraits, etc.
I. Mason, David, date.

GV1785.K28S77   792.8'092'4   C78-001215-1

CONTENTS

Designed by Richard Whyte

Colour separations by Herzig Somerville Limited

Printed and bound by The Bryant Press Limited

To my wife Maggie, whose strength and belief were everything.

D.S.

David Street and I have worked together closely on this book. He has captured many beautiful, fleeting moments of my dance and my life with the sensitivity of a great artist.

KAREN KAIN

FOREWORD

To call Karen Kain a natural dancer is perhaps a little unfair. She has worked as hard as any dancer, possibly a little harder than most, to achieve the Karen Kain we see today. Yet it is her awareness, and ability to absorb and retain, matched with an instinctive musicality, which give the ballerina her special authority and distinction.

Intelligence and musicality are by no means Karen Kain's only qualities. The beautiful photographs in this book reveal the refinement of her line and bearing and the radiance of personality which make her such a versatile and richly communicative artist.

A very celebrated dancer-choreographer once said to Karen during a particularly long and exhausting rehearsal: "I am longing for a drink. Aren't you?" She, thinking he had said: "I am longing for you to shrink," replied with some alarm: "I know you are, but there is nothing I can do about it."

She need not have worried. Karen Kain will continue to grow and grow. For what she does she was meant to do quite naturally.

Alexander Grant

When I grow Up

When I grow up I am going to be a Ballerina. I could go out every night and dace. I will be in Giselle. It will be so much fun being a Ballerina.

From school exercise book, "A Story About Me."

KAREN

For a simple and special reason, the biographical details of Karen Kain's life are briefly told. She was born one of four children to Mr. and Mrs. Charles Kain of Hamilton, Ontario. She went to her local school, and when she was nine was taken by her mother as a birthday treat to the ballet, where she saw Celia Franca dance Giselle. The spectacle fired her imagination, and her mother treasures to this day the diary in which Karen wrote the stark declaration, "I am going to be a ballerina."

She took classes near her home, auditioned successfully for the National Ballet School, and progressed well enough to become a member of the *corps de ballet* of the National Ballet of Canada. Peter Wright of the Royal Ballet saw her dance, plucked her out of the *corps de ballet* to take the lead in The Mirror Walkers, and before long she was appointed a principal ballerina with the company.

That is the bare unexciting background. No dramatic defections across international frontiers; no sudden leap to stardom; no fierce struggle with grinding poverty. It may not be the stuff of which biographies are made. Yet the reason her life is simple and outwardly unexciting is more fascinating than any dramatized and over-embellished "fairy-tale."

That reason is, quite simply, ballet.

One of the clichés of ballet that teachers stress to intending novitiates and their parents is the intense dedication required of the profession they are about to enter. It's a tough life, they say, only to be undertaken by those willing to devote themselves to it. Karen Kain has taken that cliché, absorbed it, recast it, and raised it to the level of religious dogma. Any ballet lover or critic searching for the reasons for her success will uncover a rich vein of clues in her total, all-excluding dedication to the ballet.

In basic terms, dedication means, for Karen, six or more hours a day, six days a week, working to improve her dancing. A performance falls as an additional weight on the schedule, committing her to extra hours at the theatre in advance of the curtain, for make-up, exercises, and warm-up. A dancer who goes on cold runs grave risk of an accident; consequently, Karen is often tired even before the performance starts.

Of course there is the seventh day, traditionally a day of diversion and pleasure. Not for Karen Kain. For her it is a day of rest: positive, active rest, deliberately shaped to allow muscles to recover their tension, ligaments to ease, and nerve systems to recuperate from six hard days of work and stress.

The rest day may include a visit to a masseuse, often a call on the doctor, or an hour with that new miracle worker of the athlete's world, the chiropractor. Beyond that relaxation is normally limited to a quiet supper with friends—never a big meal (dancers are as circumscribed by their career-long diet as jockeys) and never a late night. It is a merciless regime, and in it the day of rest is sacrosanct. Recently Karen and her longtime partner Frank Augustyn were invited to dance on a Toronto television network's Monday show, and offered a lucrative fee. They turned it down: "We didn't want to dance on our rest day," they said. "It might have led to a poor performance later that week."

Dedication alone, of course, is not enough to raise a dancer out of the ranks of the ordinary. One must look deeper into the artistic personality and physical capacity to discover what talent carries a dancer to the heights that Karen Kain routinely achieves. What is the nature of that achievement? What makes Karen Kain the kind of dancer she is? Indeed what kind of dancer—and person—is she?

The fact that such questions are not easily answered is what makes Karen virtually unique. In purely physical terms she is quite tall for a dancer, a fact which gives her anxieties amounting in the opinion of some of her colleagues to a complex. She tends to overlook the fact that several other ballerinas are taller than she is, and male dancers are also becoming taller and stronger. Her body is long, her hands perhaps surprisingly large. She has long black hair customarily pinned into a tight bun, green eyes, full lips. Her voice is light and her manner gentle, with a complete absence of the toughness one might expect in view of the harsh treatment she metes out to herself.

Off stage she walks with a deliberate, measured tread, feet turned markedly out, a legacy of years of training. Her clothes are fine but unobtrusive—middle-of-the-road almost—and devoid of the artistic extravagance familiar among ballet people. She might be a bank or business executive, and passes easily among the smart young professional women who work in Toronto's downtown financial buildings, close by the ballet's performing home at the O'Keefe Centre.

In terms of physical, mental, and spiritual components, Karen Kain is a remarkably normal young citizen of Ontario's metropolitan capital. The difference begins to show when she puts those components together to meet the requirements of that most ambiguous of art forms, the ballet.

If the quality of Karen's dancing can be summarized in a single word, it must be 'range'. But that hardly covers the many facets of her ability, like the extraordinary physical strength her body needs to sustain the work-load and pressures of the dancing life, nor the suppleness that brings her grace and style. Nor does it hold the key to that almost intractable problem of what distinguishes the exceptional performer from the anonymous members of the *corps de ballet*, competent, highly trained, and hard working though they may be. It is not merely the highly charged energy that she infuses into her roles, nor the richness of acting interpretation that conveys the layers of meaning in the unfolding drama, nor the sheer athleticism which combines with exquisitely feminine beauty to give ballet its unique quality. It is the mystical magical touch with a divine brush that turns all these facets of the art into mere working tools, then adds a margin of inspiration on top of that to single out the great from the merely good. It is that extra quality

which sends a ripple of spontaneous applause through an audience when Karen Kain appears on stage, which tells them the moment they see her that the entertainment for which they have paid will no longer be stamped with the mark of ordinariness. It is a quality for which the English language has only one word, though that word is not comfortably applied to this art form, so divorced from the intellectual and cerebral worlds of the other creative arts. But Karen Kain undoubtedly has it: genius.

That pedantic and pedestrian definition of genius attributed to Thomas Alva Edison—"one per cent inspiration and ninety-nine per cent perspiration"—might have been coined for the ballet in its literal sense. It is in the sweat of the class and rehearsal that the dancer's basic working tool, the body, is forged and honed for daily use. On the hour, punctually in line with theatrical practice, the dancers line up for the merciless routine of steps and movements formalized in a century-and-a-half of use as the basis for the finished art form. Ballet is one of the few arts that have retained their classical groundwork. Today's child learns piano without the grind of scales. A writer no longer needs command of the grammar of his language, still less its latin antecedents. And laborious copying of old masters is held to be stultifying for the embryonic painter. But the dancer of the 1970s starts with the same basic training that nurtured Pavlova and Nijinsky. And still the ballet master calls his dancers to perform the same sequences of movements, left side, right side, the same endless repetitions with few variations.

There is no escape, no relief, no distinction or privilege conferred by status or rank. All are anonymous, all subservient to the ballet master's call. The same dusty studio in downtown Toronto echoes to the same strident piano, and somewhere in the middle of the massed ranks of sweating figures in darned tights, plastic slimsuits, vests and leotards, Nureyev and Kain are striving to keep their bodies conditioned and tuned for the rehearsal which will follow, and the performance which will follow all too hard upon that later in the day.

"It is sheer drudgery," Karen condemns class with a distasteful expression.

She has not been reminded of that other old aphorism, more illuminating than Edison's, that defines the genuineness of a calling according to how much a person enjoys the drudgery of their profession. Whatever she says, Karen enjoys the sheer drudgery of her dancing. She is as dedicated to preparing for the ballet as she is to performing it. Before being called to the *barre* by the ballet mistress she spends several minutes in stretching and warming exercises. From then on her work is as perfect as she can make it.

In a small class at the old St. Lawrence Hall with Rudolf Nureyev and colleagues Tomas Schramek and Mary Jago, she is compact, correct, unobtrusive: she stands out by way of her very anonymity. It is one of the many unfathomable contradictions in her character, that the performer whose stage personality is so commanding should be so utterly self-effacing in class. Schramek is vibrant, brilliant: Mary Jago elegant and statuesque. Nureyev, master showman, dominates the proceedings, trudging aside for a towel, changing his clothes as his body warms, losing his woollen bonnet, swearing foully in English at the distracting click of a camera.

Karen has been scarcely visible, needing no correction from the ballet mistress, asking for no attention, making no demands. She is simply here to practice, and patiently, introspectively concentrates on giving every movement her total devotion.

It is another aspect of her dedication. In terms of Karen's own view of her work her personality is of little consequence. There is no ego at work claiming identification or adulation. All that counts is the quality of the dancing, and even if the infinite repetitions are tedious, the movements themselves are supremely important, each one an object to be polished to perfection for its own sake.

You can see the same approach in rehearsal, especially in the dress rehearsal. "A good dancer must be able to mark," said the teacher Agnes de Mille. *Mark* is a ballet term which describes the process of going through the steps at half-pitch, partly using the hands to simulate the feet movements, in order to set the dance into the physical part of the memory without the exertion of all-out effort. Karen does very little of it. It is almost sacrilegious to her way of moving to give less than one hundred per cent.

The girls in the *corps de ballet* may mark, walking with apparent laziness when the steps are light and graceful. The sharp rebuke from the ballet mistress echoes round the auditorium: "Walk properly girls, not on your heels."

It is inconceivable that Karen would ever receive such admonition.

"You never go full out in rehearsal," she says.

But she is being barely honest. The result is that you can see dancing from Karen as intensely transporting in rehearsal as you see in performance. Her fellow principals may halt the ballet to re-run the steps. Karen moves steadily forward, free of fuss, dedicated as ever to attaining the unattainable—that elusive perfection of movement, the search for which is the hallmark of everything she does.

One memorable occasion she did allow herself a minor lapse from her own standard. It was a dour March evening, and a dress rehearsal for Sleeping Beauty. To liven up the uneventful proceedings Karen put on bright blue leg warmers, a wig borrowed from the witch Carabosse, and horn-rimmed glasses, and in this extraordinary costume lay on her bed, waiting for the Prince's kiss. Unsuspecting, Frank Augustyn danced round the stage, unable to understand the titters from the company until he arrived at the bedside, to be confronted—and momentarily halted—by the hideously transformed vision. It was an innocent joke and amused everybody. But it rebounded.

"I got into trouble the next day for indiscipline," Karen recalls. "They said I should not set a bad example to the younger dancers."

It is hard to conceive a more disciplined performer, nor one who could be held as a better example for a young dancer to follow. It is even harder to deny a star a rare indulgence.

Apart from her compulsive search for perfection in the dance itself, Karen Kain is motivated by one other force in her performance of the ballet, the desire to carry the message to the people of her country.

16

It would be easy for Karen to leave Toronto behind and develop a lucrative career on the international circuit. A season here, a guest appearance there: the airport lounge and hotel room are the environment which sustains many an artist of stature today.

Already she has been acclaimed in a dozen capitals and other major cities around the world. New York, Moscow, Chicago, London, Paris, San Francisco, Melbourne, Sydney, Vienna, Marseilles—all have seen her work and would welcome her back for longer bookings. The honours, including prizes in Moscow and appearances with the Bolshoi Ballet, have come readily. Yet she retains a modest loyalty, both to the city she works in and to the company of which she is a part.

"Toronto is my home," she says. "I like the city and would not like to leave it permanently. Also I was brought up in this company. I'm happy with them. I like the people and the work we do here. I don't want to move away."

At the same time she knows that ballet is a youthful art as far as Canada is concerned, and there are elements of missionary zeal in her regard for the Canadian people.

"I want us to be able to communicate as dancers with men and women who do not normally patronize the ballet. We have to abolish the idea that the ballet is for an elite. I want the construction worker and the taxi driver to be able to come in and appreciate what is going on."

For this reason she also carries a self-imposed burden of responsibility if she does not get the message over to those who come to watch. When an audience is cold and unresponsive Karen blames herself for failing to inspire their enthusiasm. Similarly she considers it her duty as an actress in the dance to transmit the message of the ballet in her actions and mime.

This regard for the audience is a central element in the outlook of any successful dancer. The ballet is an illusion, and both spectator and performer must enter into it to complete the theatrical experience. The dancer's part in the illusion depends on her ability to disguise from the audience, like a conjuror, the mechanics which make possible that which we believed to be unattainable.

In ballet, this idea can be reduced to one simple truth: the beauty in movement that you see on stage is a function of the daunting, exhausting physical effort expended, both in class and in performance. The audience may not know it, and if they do know it they must be made to forget it, but the dancer who creates mobile images in front of them does so at the expense of burning, screaming pain in the muscles and joints, frequent cramps, almost perpetually blistered feet, and searing torment in the lungs and throat.

Like any athlete, the ability to suffer degrees of pain such as these comes only from incessant training, and an unconquerable determination to drive on through the obstacles to achieve of the body's ultimate capabilities. There is one difference. The athlete is permitted to sweat, spit, gasp, roll his head, and collapse at the end of his effort. The dancer may not. Her task requires that she must suppress these instincts, and maintain the illusion of detached calm, total physical composure, and freedom from ordinary human reaction.

"That," says Karen with brutal simplicity, "is the difference between sport and art."

It is one of the long-debated contentions in music whether a technical understanding of the construction of the piece adds materially to the enjoyment of the listener. The same arguments could be ranged on each side with regard to the ballet. Should an audience know the mechanical composition, perhaps the names in French, of the series of steps that form a *pas de deux* or soloist's variation? Would their enjoyment be enhanced if they knew, perhaps by trying them, the technical difficulties of some of the basic jumps and steps and turns in the dancer's repertoire?

Perhaps their appreciation of the total beauty unfolding in movement before them might be more poignant if they were aware that when Karen Kain returns to the stage after her partner's lift with the grace and softness of a snowflake falling in slow motion, she is doing so by virtue of the iron hard muscle in calf and thigh: that when she performs a *pas de bourré* to travel across the stage *en pointe* with the poise of a sea-horse, it is at the expense of inhuman stress on instep and ankle, and unbearable chafing of the feet from unfamiliar shoes which wear out before they ever have time to be worn in.

And it would be no more than justice to the dancer if sometimes, just occasionally, critics with a facility for dismissing her efforts, and audiences who feel cheated if they fail to be touched by magic, would visualize the scene backstage when a dancer goes off. When, for example, Karen has just danced the great act three variation from Swan Lake, she floats away into the wings as if suspended on air. The moment she is out of sight of the audience she doubles at the waist to get back the loss of breath, falls flat on her heels to take the strain out of her legs, and whips a tissue from the company box to wipe away runnels of sweat from her face and shoulders. In bodies conditioned to an advanced state of fitness a few deep gasping breaths rapidly restore the oxygen supply to heaving lungs, and in seconds the dancer composes herself. The mask of concentration once more covers the strained and sweating features. The body rises visible inches on re-tensioned muscles. The illusion is about to be restored. The dancer is ready for her next entrance.

A dancer's body is as fit as any athlete's or boxer's (in Karen's words, "It goes far beyond fitness.") yet dancers are not anxious that the audience should recognize the pain and strain. "They don't come to watch ordinary athletes," says Karen. "They come to be transported out of their daily lives. Part of my job is to preserve that illusion for them."

Even so, when at the end of an enchanting variation, we are inclined to applaud the spectacle we have just seen, it might be worth letting our minds dwell on the struggle with wracking exhaustion taking place in the wings. And perhaps we could spare a small portion of our applause not solely for the beauty of the dance, but for the extent of the purely physical achievement.

Many people, dancers among them, use their work as a means to an end. They trade hours of work for hours of leisure. They use the money they earn to follow other pursuits. They buy fast sports cars, set up fabulous mansions, take skiing holidays, eat in expensive restaurants, even touch the fringes of politics. They accumulate acquisitions which they hope will boost their personal identity outside their work, and build up a public persona that will carry them through the deficiencies of their talent, possibly even overcome the indifference of a fickle public.

Not so Karen Kain. Her dedication to the ballet is such that any activity or major interest outside it would detract from her absorption in her work. So she allows herself no such indulgences.

She owns no car. In fact she has never learned to drive. Her knowledge of her own adopted city is sketchy, and she might find difficulty in navigating herself around it. When she steps into a cab at the O'Keefe Centre or St. Lawrence Hall and announces her destination, she switches off. Finding the way home is the driver's job. Hers is dancing. And that is sufficient.

Even the usual reward of the travelling artist, a comfortable familiarity with the world's capitals, is denied to Karen. Wherever she may be, her world is bounded by the studio and theatre. The demands of her work mean that travel, real travel in the form of immersion in the fascinating world that she has glimpsed but never truly embraced, remains a distant dream. A rare holiday is a three-week break for sunshine, sea and sand somewhere like Antigua. But like the weekly day-off, a holiday serves a positive purpose. It is a device for recuperation and reconditioning the body and spirit, not mere reward for a year's work.

If Karen allows herself any form of escape from the demands of her profession it is simply relaxing at home. A day spent quietly pottering around the house, much of it curled up in a favourite chair with a good book, provides the right antithesis to her work.

Home for Karen is a small house in Cabbagetown, a district of downtown Toronto where the city's middleclass professionals have been snapping up dilapidated Victorian and Edwardian properties and gutting and restoring them, bringing them through the full cycle of opulence, decay and devastation, and back to opulence. Cabbagetown is again a picturesque district where the patina of age and modern architectural technology provide a highly desirable escape from the dreary uniformity of the outer suburbs.

Karen's house, shared with her sister Sandy who is a nurse, provides the perfect background to her forays into the Canadian and international dancing scenes. Outside, it is a small cottage-like brick house, unassuming but attractive. Indoors, it has been structurally rearranged by a Canadian architect with a three-dimensional outlook. He has abandoned the conventional ground and upper floors and opened out rooms to give a high vaulted ceiling, a gallery, and steps down to a pine kitchen—a multi-level home where the essentials of Canadian modernity lie comfortably alongside the traditional soaring effects of a cathedral. Karen's furnishings are well chosen and match her personality—elegant, free of fuss, quality without ostentation. Apart from being an investment, a financial buffer against a dancer's uncertain long-term future, Karen's house is a hobby, to be cultivated, furnished, re-decorated.

At a more profound level it is an anchor, a refuge, a place for quiet contemplation, calm and restorative in its atmosphere like a medieval church. In fact the religious allusion is not inappropriate. Karen's life is one of almost religious commitment. Like any nun she has taken her vows when young, and follows her calling with a nun's devotion, going through the same ritualistic routines aimed at achieving the same sublime, if humble, perfection. In her case the rituals are not prayer and devotions, but exercises, class, rehearsals, and performance.

But then the enigmatic contradictions in her character arise again. Frequently in people of such a religious disposition there is a long-term aim, with every activity moulded towards its achievement. Often it is called a career. Karen has little conception of a career. Her approach is entirely pragmatic, her vision deliberately short: today's rehearsal, tomorrow's performance,

yesterday's achievement ruthlessly analyzed. Perhaps the short view is itself the mark of the true artist: the work in hand is all absorbing; tomorrow's task can look after itself.

The same pragmatic approach dominates her private life. Her outlook is entirely unsentimental, utterly logical. The press are given to asking attractive young women at the peak of their careers about marriage, drawing pictures of a beautiful ballerina linked with a successful young lawyer or diplomat. Alternatively they run up romantic images—Karen and a male dancer sharing a domestic partnership alongside their artistic one. To Karen such ideas are incomprehensible; they raise lines of puzzlement on her brow. "How can I know what kind of man I will marry?" she asks. "He could follow any profession. All that matters is that we should want to marry. I'll marry the right man. That's all."

Her mind, like her life, is free from frills. And it is a great advantage. It allows her total concentration on her work. No doubt it is why she is at the top.

Almost all the great dancers have been given a label of some kind by their critics or their most appreciative fans. This one is a lyrical dancer, that one has purity of line: a certain dancer has exceptional technique, another fine interpretation.

Karen Kain confounds categorization. She is an accomplished and powerful actress, whose search for interesting characterization and informative interpretation is sincere and diligent. Her facial expression and mime are as eloquent as can be achieved within the limitations of this theater-without-words. The transformation of Giselle from the cheerful peasant girl, flirting lovingly with her admirer, into the demented and betrayed suicide shows qualities of inner conviction that would credit a dramatic actress of some stature.

As for the mechanics of dancing, her command is so that it would be invidious to select particular accomplishments: the process would unjustly omit others. Yet certain striking visual images remain in the mind, impressing their authority on the viewer.

Consider for example the final moments of Swan Lake, when the lamenting Swan Queen's wings beat gently as the curtain falls. There is a lucidity and suppleness of movement in Karen Kain's arms that defies the division into rigid humerus, radius and ulna, carpals, metacarpals, and phalanges.

Or take the series of thirty-two *fouetté* turns danced by the same performer as Odile in that ballet. They present an athletic, almost acrobatic challenge that even Margot Fonteyn confessed caused her problems. Karen produces them with the whip and precision of a machine turning out metal components.

Watch her *arabesque*, where her balance and equilibrium *en pointe* give the impression that she could hold it indefinitely, with none of the visible shifting corrections that most performers require. Or take that other extraordinary feat of balance, the *rose adage*, in which the ballerina is supported in *arabesque* by her partner, releases him to touch her hands above her head, and lowers her hand after the briefest interval to regain his support. In bullfighting (an activity with strange

"I still get terribly nervous before a performance. The only way I can cope with this is to stop trying to live up to other people's expectations of me and try to live up to my own."

affinities with ballet) there is a moment in the final act when the matador advances on the bull for the kill. As he drives the sword he is poised for a brief but perceptible interval above the bull's horns, vulnerable to a reflex upward thrust. It is called the 'moment of truth.' Second rate matadors can simulate it: great ones display the unmistakable authentic version. It is the same in ballet. The equilibrium can be simulated, or can be shown as perfectly controlled—a pure 'moment of truth.' Karen shows that control almost every time she dances, leaving the impression that she could hold the position without her partner's support for a substantial margin longer than the dance requires.

But technical dissection of this dancer's art is no service to the magic of her ability, nor to her colossal and towering technique. Roland Petit, who created Nana for Karen to perform with the Paris Opéra Company, is as well placed as any critic to summarize Karen's ability. He expresses it perfectly: "Karen Kain is a choreographer's dream," he says. "She can do anything you ask her to."

If her devotion to the classical parts is thorough and comprehensive, her appetite for exploring the opportunities of modern ballet display another facet of her true artist's nature. All the time, Karen is seeking to extend her work in the dance. And if the performance of Giselle or Coppélia dominate one week in the season, then it is no contradiction that she should be simultaneously engaged in a brooding and violent Canadian modern ballet like Mad Shadows, the exuberant Kettentanz, or the graphic and vibrant Four Schumann Pieces.

As artistic director of the National Ballet of Canada, Alexander Grant and his staff are striving to build up the company's repertoire to cover the entire spectrum of classical and modern works. Only by that means can a young company establish and consolidate an international reputation, or attract a home audience without relying on the pulling power of visiting superstars. In that plan Karen Kain and dancers like her are a vital component, dancers with the technical equipment to take on the heavy load of learning roles throughout the range, and with the artistic personality to stamp those roles with their own individual vision. Fortunately Karen has a great facility for memorizing new roles, as well as an open-minded approach to the intentions of choreographers and ballet masters with whom she works, fulfilling another of Agnes de Mille's requirements for a good dancer, that she must be 'teachable.'

Karen faces two major problems in her work. The first arises, insidiously and unseen, from the very fact of her total command of her art. For a dancer who finds new work so easy to assimilate, and who by her early twenties has danced almost all of the great classical roles, the great danger lies in the rarity of a new challenge. It would be perfectly possible for her to run out of enthusiasm.

David Scott, ballet master for her company, recognizes this problem: "She is a dancer of great intelligence, and she needs feeding something new in artistic terms. The great classical ballets provide a renewable challenge through their fusion of technical demands with opportunities for artistic interpretation, both balletic and dramatic. She also needs new modern roles, perpetually adding to the variety of stimulus in her work."

Fortunately Karen herself also recognizes the danger, but she is modest enough to know that after working on a modern ballet she can—and must—return to the classical roles for the discipline and demand they provide. "It is like putting on a hair shirt," she says. "You go back to do the work all over again, seeking new ways to find the technical perfection the roles demand."

Roland Petit, who knows Karen's potential as well as any choreographer, sees the same problem from another angle. His judgment is that she must pace herself through her career: "Her skill is like a jewel. She must take care of it, and not spend her treasure too fast."

At the time of writing Karen is in her mid-twenties, a watershed in the life of anyone whose profession depends on athletic ability. By the time they reach Karen's age some of her colleagues have already given up their work in ballet to concentrate on carving out the remainder of their careers in areas not limited by physical decline. Those at the top who continue to dance might expect another ten or fifteen years before the body refuses to perform as the mind wills it to. Exceptionally, a handful of dancers like Pavlova and Margot Fonteyn defy the years, making marginal adjustments in technique and compensating for them by their wealth of experience and artistic maturity. Without doubt Karen has the technical equipment to go on dancing almost indefinitely, or at least so long as her hunger to do so remains keen. Alternatively she might emerge as a teacher, or move into acting.

Perhaps the answer to the future for Karen lies in that delicately orchestrated counterpoint between the excitement of new work, and the dwindling but increasingly demanding opportunities for polishing and reinterpreting the traditional dances.

"She could go on doing that for the next twenty years," says David Scott.

In which case the longevity of Fonteyn and Pavlova may prove to be far less exceptional than generally thought.

Whether the next two decades will see an increasing devotion to the ballet, or an application of her talent to some completely different field of expression, may prove to be one of the most interesting themes in Canadian art in the foreseeable future.

Karen's other problem lies in the modern artistic paradox, that art is not sufficient in itself. She cannot accept that in a world dominated by the media, insatiable in its appetite for scandal above quality, sheer Olympian ability is not enough. To be an artist is to court obscurity. Allied to talent must be media appeal, which involves publicity sense. It may have been accidental that Nureyev and Fonteyn were busted at a California drugs party, but they made the most of the publicity generated by the event.

Karen's chief problem is that she has a fundamentally pleasant disposition. She is not excited by the idea of stardom, nor can she simulate the abrasive, difficult, obstructionist character that today seems a prerequisite for public attention. She still seems amazed at her luck in being singled out for several curtain calls at the end of a ballet. And she still takes immense delight in receiving flowers, taking home every bouquet to be cherished for as long as it lasts.

It is yet another aspect of the ambivalence in Karen Kain which is at the root of her fascination, both personal and professional: the innocent, unassuming girl who achieves miracles of artistic expression.

The combination is irresistible, and the conclusion inescapable. Whether she is on stage working or at home washing dishes, Karen Kain cannot help being beautiful.

"I never tire of hearing applause. All artists need a constant reaffirmation of their value to the public, because they are always insecure and need to know that they are still loved. In many ways it is the only reward for the hard work.

"Of course there is the personal satisfaction in accomplishing things that the audience wouldn't know about—little things like a certain control in your technique. But to know that they have appreciated your efforts makes it all worthwhile."

The BARRE

(Overleaf) At the barre with Joanne Nisbet, Rudolf Nureyev and Tomas Schramek.

"The morning class, starting at the barre, is the one constant of dance. The ballets change and you work with different choreographers with different demands, but the barre exercises remain the same day after day, over and over. The strain is tremendous because you keep making your body do things it doesn't want to do naturally."

"Rehearsal is everything. Constant, constant rehearsal. Always trying to improve your technique, striving for a certain perfection. You rehearse until your muscles hurt and until the fatigue makes your legs feel as though they have lead weights in them. You do it though, because you know without it your performance will suffer."

JAZZ

"The music is what makes me dance. I try to interpret what the music is saying to me. Although I find the greatest challenge in classical ballet, I do not want to limit myself to that. I love ballroom dancing, I adore waltzing. If the music is a jazz rhythm, then that's the kind of movement I want to do to it."

*Rehearsal for the André Gagnon C.B.C. Superspecial, choreographed by Brian MacDonald.
Dancers Tomas Schramek, Victor Edwards, David Fornik and Robert Derosiers.*

LADY of DANCE

"I have always loved to dance. When I was a little girl I used to put records on and dance by myself in the basement of our home. It seems now that I was either sitting down or I was dancing. Of course I had no idea of the amount of energy and dedication that would be involved. I just danced because I loved it."

"I was about fifteen years old, I think, when I realized I was really addicted to dancing, that it was my way of life. I was at the National Ballet School and sometimes life was very difficult. I remember terrible bouts of homesickness and self-consciousness about my weight and the

braces on my teeth! I don't think I made any great sacrifices to go there, though. I had a purpose to my young life, I knew what I wanted to do and all my energies were channeled in that direction. I never sat around wondering what I was going to do when I grew up."

"I still love to go back to the school to visit. Whenever I need to brush up on my technique I can take a class with Betty Oliphant, the principal of the school, or Daniel Seillier, one of my favourite teachers. The studios are marvellous there with large church windows and beautiful wooden floors. The young students seem to be in awe of me and ask me for autographs and I remember when I used to do exactly the same thing."

SWAN LAKE

"Swan Lake is in many ways the traditionalist's ballet and it has always been very special for me because it was my first big role and my first success. It is an exhausting ballet to perform, not only because it is very demanding physically but there is the extra challenge involved in portraying the spiritual side of Odette, the white swan, and the sensual side of Odile, the black swan. The music never ceases to inspire me. It is very emotional. I still feel tears in my eyes and shivers up my spine as the final chords are played."

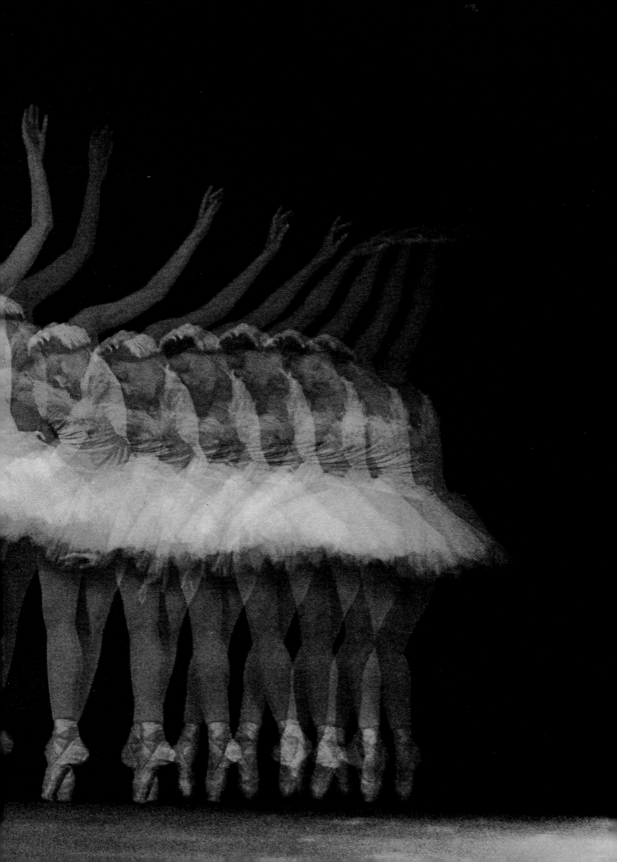

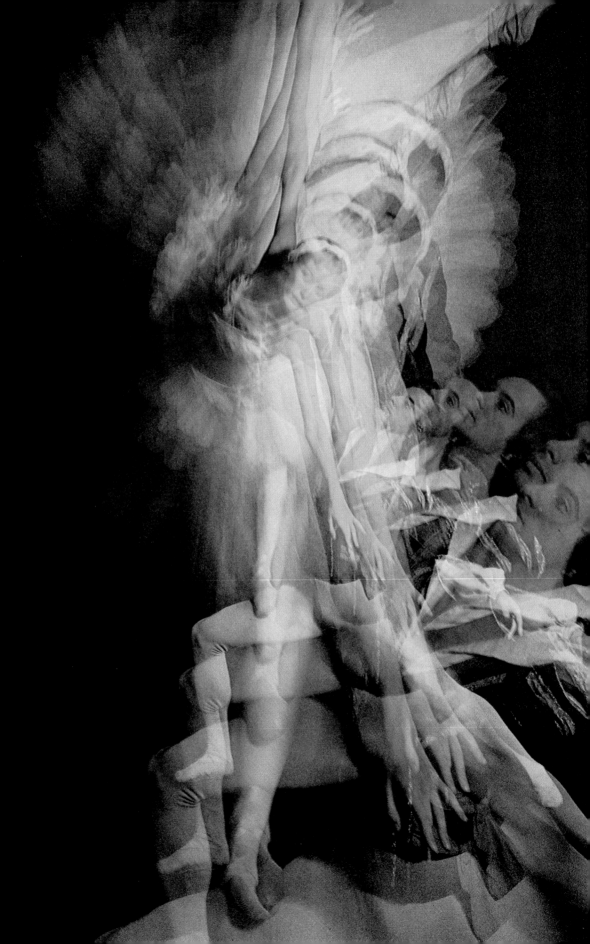

"Frank Augustyn and I seem to have developed a very special rapport and in Swan Lake this is especially important because the ballet consists mainly of *pas de deux* and I have to rely a great deal on my partner. I get that extra bit of confidence about a performance when I know I will be dancing with him."

MAD SHADOWS

"Mad Shadows, a new ballet choreographed by my good friend Ann Ditchburn
to music by André Gagnon, was something altogether new to me. The character I
played, Louise, an older woman in love with her son, went beyond the boundaries
of dance. It was a strenuous acting role unlike anything I had ever tried before.
The *pas de deux* danced by Louise and her lover Lanz practically demanded acrobatic
training. I would come off stage black and blue with bruises.

"It is important for an artist to remain open to change and influence.
In other words to be versatile. Never to be open to new things, new ideas, is to remain
too safe."

AFTERNOON of a FAUN

"Afternoon of a Faun is a beautiful *pas de deux* by Jerome Robbins about the blossoming of young love between two dancers practicing in the studio. The music is by Debussy and the atmosphere that is created, if it is done well, can be spellbinding."

"Nureyev is an inspiration to anyone who watches him work. His devotion to dance is total. Sometimes I think he is almost superhuman because he works so hard and tires long after everyone else. He is an incredible artist and a good friend who has gone out of his way to help me."

Karen rehearsing with Rudolf Nureyev, watched by David Scott, dancemaster of the National Ballet of Canada.

CORSAIR

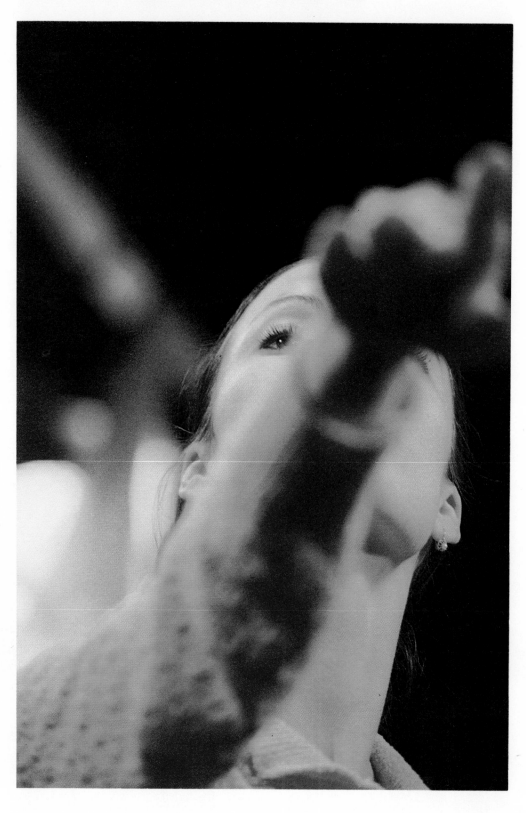

Conversations

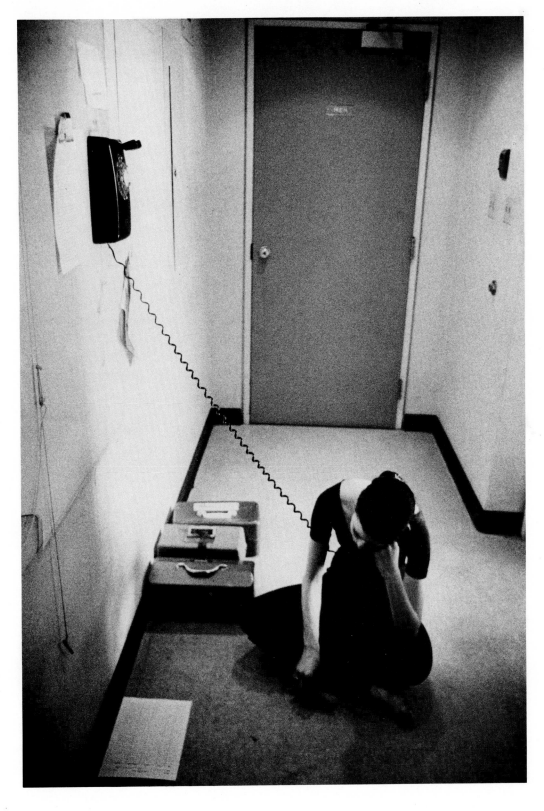

"People often say to me that it must be exciting to have a famous sister. It just seems natural. I never really considered, all of a sudden, that Karen was famous. It's just that even when she was in ballet school I assumed she would have to be good because just about everything that happened around her was always special. I expected it. I would have been disappointed if it had turned out any other way."

SANDY KAIN

"I find working with Karen can be fabulous—we have a bit of *sympatico* going on. I know when not to push her for interviews and so forth, but Karen is one of the few principals who realize that I am under pressure too and she'll do things for me even though I know she is working hard and I don't want to ask her. She understands her responsibility as a prima ballerina; it is a role that you have to play and I think Karen knows this and isn't intimidated by it.

"We have gone off to New York and other places together for press interviews and believe me we've been through a few traumatic things, but we laugh about it. She is like that; somehow around Karen you feel good.

"Probably the greatest admiration I have is for her musicality—it's enigmatic. She is technically one of the strongest dancers but she has this special grace behind her technique. That is really the magic of her dance. I am in constant awe of her when I see her dance, whether in rehearsal or performance. The maturity and professionalism—there never seems to be a moment when she lets up on herself. She is an easy person, fun, she has a terrific sense of humour when she is sitting on the side but the moment she gets up to dance everything seems blocked out. It is a very special concentration and again that is another quality that makes a ballerina great and Karen has got it."

GERRI CIMINO,
ASSISTANT PUBLICITY DIRECTOR,
NATIONAL BALLET OF CANADA

Dear Miss Kain,

I am writing this letter to thank you for a wonderful performance of Giselle.

I sort of wished it wouldn't end and I sort of wished it would end. I wished it wouldn't end because I simply LOVED it! I wished it would end because after the millions of curtain calls, I could sneak around to the stage door and see you! Which I did. (I don't think you remember me, the little kid with the short blonde hair and gold barret?)

I am a 10-year-old girl who thinks you are fantastic. . . .

Love:
Your fan:

BEATRICE U.

"I recognized Karen's talent at her first audition to enter the school. There was a real concern that her figure might not turn out. She was fairly overweight for a long period, although that is difficult to believe now, but it certainly didn't negate her talent. She loved to dance. I put my money on her by giving her the lead in the school's production of Swan Lake, for which I was criticized because some people felt she would be unlikely to ever dance the role on stage because of her figure. I did it though because I felt it was really important to show my confidence in her.

"She was a very headstrong young girl and very self-willed. I remember once we took the students to the ballet at Maple Leaf Gardens and the kids were *not* allowed backstage. Well we lost Karen. Nureyev was dancing and she had run away from our group. We found her eventually, hiding behind some scenery backstage, she wanted to see Nureyev so much. She was a little monkey but always very nice—she still is. She has her own honesty and she deals with herself honestly.

"Now of course she is receiving the critical acclaim she deserves. She is a very versatile dancer; she expresses herself through her body so totally. She has that tremendous fortitude. She went on in Paris once when she was seriously ill; she passed out and was rushed to hospital and operated on right away. She had a wild period a while ago when she was probably trying too much to be all things to all people. Everything that was a new experience she was grabbing at, which is not really the way to develop as an artist. She was burning herself out. But she discovered this her own way. The thing is, Karen has this marvellous love of life and wants to experience everything. She is developing a lot more artistic maturity and subtleties and nuances; she is becoming far more selective in the roles she dances and is digging even deeper into her roles.

"I don't see her ever giving up dancing because she is essentially a dancer. She might become an actress for a while or a film star but I think basically she will always have a career in ballet. Of course one never knows with Karen, she might just settle down with a family . . . no that's not Karen at all. I think she would make a *terrific* teacher one day if she wants to. Terrific. She understands dance so well."

BETTY OLIPHANT,
PRINCIPAL,
NATIONAL BALLET SCHOOL

108

"My first memory of Karen is of a girl with braces and small ears. I was not, however, to learn much more about her until we started performing together with the National Ballet in 1971. From that time onwards our careers and our lives have developed and progressed together. In performing we try to complement and to communicate with each other in a way that will best realize for the audience a total expression. In so doing, a sensitivity and a trust both physical and emotional have developed.

"There are certain times and certain people that seem predestined in one's life and upon reflection one cannot contemplate any other in their place. Karen holds such a place in my life."

FRANK AUGUSTYN

Backstage

"Backstage is a whole other world. It is hard to believe sometimes that magic is made from all that chaos!"

(Clockwise from top left) Entering the already crowded dressing room after a performance. With Rudolf Nureyev at the O'Keefe Centre. With Frank Augustyn and Betty Oliphant. With mother Winifred Kain.

"I love to see my family and friends after a performance, but often all the energy I have expended takes its toll and I hardly have the strength to say hello."

(Above) In Ottawa with Frank Augustyn and Margaret and Pierre Trudeau. (Below) Brother Kevin and parents Charles and Winifred Kain.

114

GISELLE

"Giselle is a beautiful ballet, a love story about a young peasant girl who discovers she has been betrayed by her lover and dies from a broken heart. In the second act she returns as a spirit to forgive him and save him from the other spirits of jilted girls who have died before their wedding day. It is certainly one of my favorite roles because it combines some of the most beautiful steps and movingly dramatic moments in any ballet. Also, being the first ballet I saw on stage, it holds a special place in my heart."

My Descripetron

I am a girl in grade three. My name is Karen Kain. I go to Fessenden school. I am eight going on nine. My eyes are hazel but I wish they were blue. My hair is dark brown Mummy says it will be pitch black when I grow up. I weight is 64 pounds. My height is 4 ft 7. I am allright middlesize. I hope to be a nice person all my life.

From school exercise book, "A Story About Me."

ACKNOWLEDGEMENTS

As with any book this one reached fruition through the help and cooperation of a number of people.

I would especially like to thank writer David Mason for his ability to interpret Karen's lifestyle while so complementing my photographs; and thank you to his wife Patricia for her support.

Thank you to Richard Whyte for the many hours of happy collaboration in designing the book.

Thank you to Frank Augustyn, for his patience and cooperation.

I would also like to thank: Rudolf Nureyev, Alexander Grant, David Scott and Joanne Nisbet, Gerri Cimino, Ann Ditchburn, the principal dancers and *corps de ballet* of the National Ballet of Canada, Paul Raymond for his makeup, Craig Allen for his advice, the Canadian Broadcasting Corporation, the O'Keefe Centre, Toronto, the National Arts Centre, Ottawa, I.A.T.S.E., and, for their fine colour work, BGM Colour Laboratories, Toronto.

Finally special thanks to Charles and Winifred Kain and their family.

FOOTNOTE

This book started when I went backstage after seeing Karen Kain perform and said to her that I wanted to photograph a book on her. She replied simply, "Oh. Do you? That's great." We never really looked back. It was far from easy. There seemed to be innumerable obstacles but in retrospect none were too great.

To say that Karen Kain is a beautiful and incredibly talented woman seems somehow superfluous, yet I feel the truth can always be repeated. To have been able to work with her closely was an honour and an experience to be cherished. Through her I was able to love dance. I hope this book will enable others to share Karen's very special being.

DAVID STREET

"I never tire of receiving flowers."